Ludwig van Beethoven
(1770-1827)

Sonatas

Sonates

Sonaten

I

for piano • pour piano • für Klavier

Urtext

K 107

OVER 25.000 PAGES OF PIANO MUSIC SHEETS ONLINE

K 107

Bach, Beethoven, Brahms, Chopin, Czerny, Debussy, Gershwin, Dvořák, Grieg, Haydn, Joplin, Lyadov, Mendelssohn-Bartholdy, Mozart, Mussorgsky, Purcell, Schubert, Schumann, Scriabin, Tchaikovsky and many more

KÖNEMANN

© 2016 koenemann.com GmbH
www.koenemann.com

Editor: István Máriássy
Responsible co-editor: Tamás Záskaliczky
Technical editor: Dezső Varga
Engraved by Kottamester Bt., Budapest

ISBN 978-3-7419-1426-3

Printed in Spain by LitoStamp

INDEX

Sonate Op. 2., No. 1.	4
Sonate Op. 2., No. 2.	20
Sonate Op. 2., No. 3.	44
Grande Sonate Op. 7.	72
Sonate Op. 10., No. 1.	98
Sonate Op. 10., No. 2.	112
Sonate Op. 10., No. 3.	128
Grande Sonate pathétique Op. 13.	154
Sonate Op. 14., No. 1.	176
Sonate Op. 14., No. 2.	190
Grande Sonate Op. 22.	209

Joseph Haydn gewidmet

Sonate
pour le clavecin ou pianoforte

Op. 2., No. 1.
1795

Joseph Haydn gewidmet

Sonate
pour le clavecin ou pianoforte

Op. 2., No. 2.
1795

Joseph Haydn gewidmet

Sonate
pour le clavecin ou pianoforte

Op. 2., No. 3.
1795

Der Gräfin Babette von Keglevics gewidmet

Grande Sonate
pour le clavecin ou pianoforte

Op. 7.
1796–97

Largo, con gran espressione

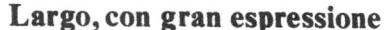

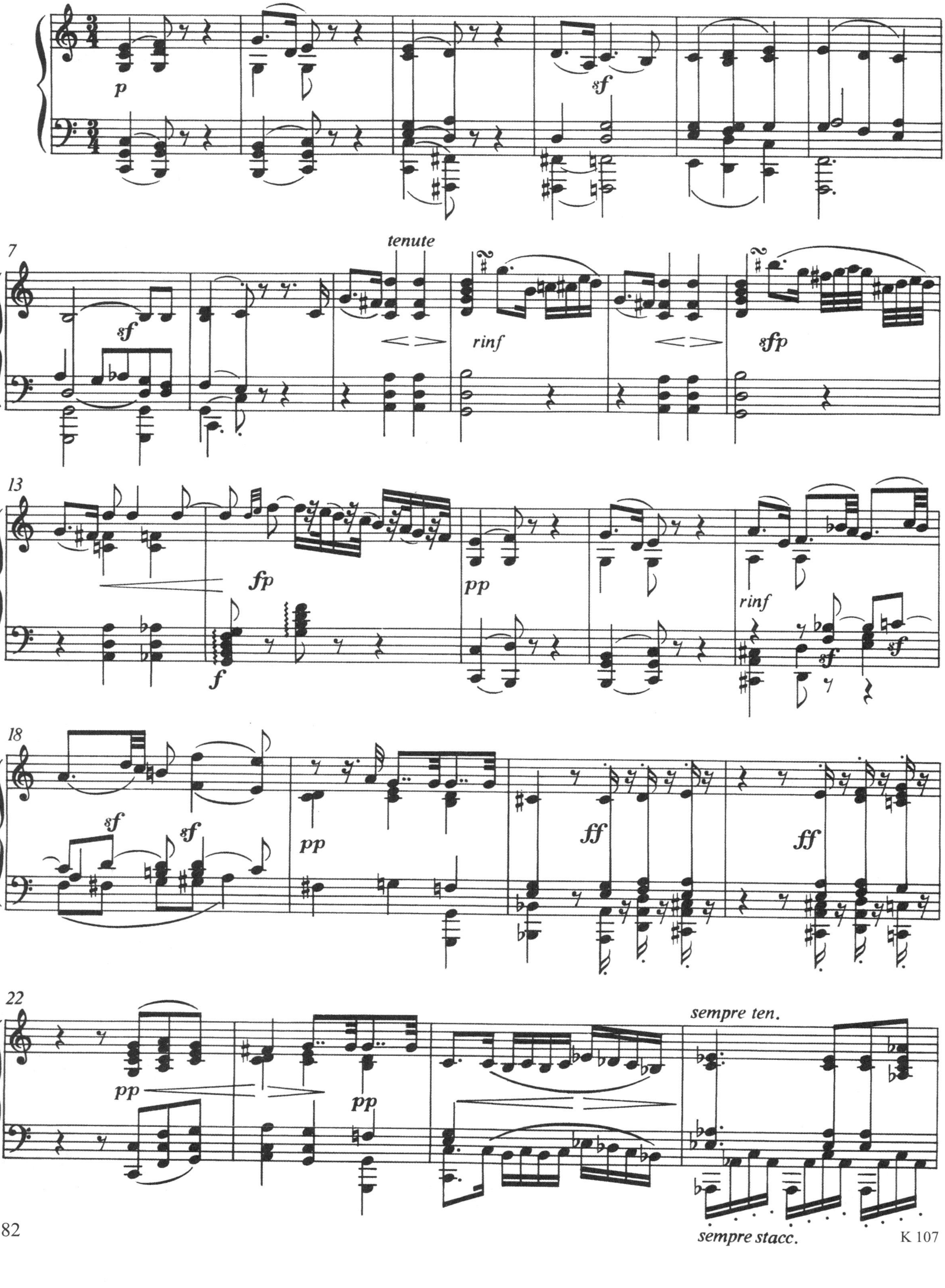

Rondo
Poco Allegretto e grazioso

Der Gräfin Anna Margarete von Browne gewidmet

Sonate
pour le clavecin ou pianoforte

Op. 10., No. 1.
1796–98

Der Gräfin Anna Margarete von Browne gewidmet

Sonate
pour le clavecin ou pianoforte

Op. 10., No. 2.
1796–98

Der Gräfin Anna Margarete von Browne gewidmet

Sonate
pour le clavecin ou pianoforte

Op. 10., No. 3.
1796–98

142

K 107

Dem Fürsten Carl von Lichnowsky gewidmet

Grande Sonate pathétique
pour le clavecin ou pianoforte

Op. 13.
1798–99

attacca subito il Allegro:

K 107

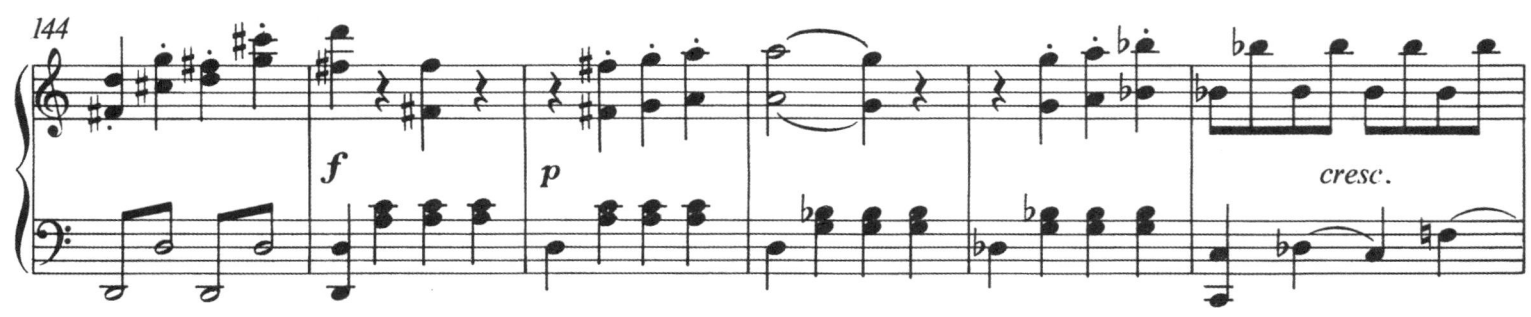

Der Baronin Josefa von Braun gewidmet

Sonate
pour le pianoforte

Op. 14., No. 2.
1798–99

10.

Dem Grafen Johann Georg von Browne gewidmet

Grande Sonate
pour le pianoforte

Op. 22.
1799–1800

11.

216

230

K 107